THE NEWBIES GUIDE TO USING THE INTERNET

SUBTITLE

TABLE OF CONTENTS

WHY READ THIS BOOK?

I wrote this book for people who want to do productive things on the internet to help make their lives easier and better. This is not for people who use the internet all the time and use these programs and services. I work in a job where I talk to people all over the country every day dealing with computer issues and how they can do things with their computers.

I see every day how much people do not know how to use their computers and use the internet to make their lives easier and better. This book is done with simple explanations to show even a novice how to get the most out of your computers and the internet.

I set this book up to show you what you can do to make your life easier and better. I will show you enough to use the different things and get the benefit out of them. If you use it a lot, you will see other ways to use it and other things you can do if you get deeper into the specific things.

We will go through how to use the most used pieces of social media. We will go through:

- Facebook
- Twitter
- Google plus
- Instagram
- Reddit
- Tumblr

- We will also go through things like why post things on social media. What things should you post? What things you should not post. What are the best ways to communicate with the people you need and want to keep in contact with?
- We will go over the best search engines and how to use them to find what you are looking for.
- I will go over the best way to store photographs online and your computer.
- I will also go over how to save things you see online. How to use the devices you have available anytime to retrieve those things. How to use them to make your life easier and better.

- We will go over backing up the things you want to make sure you will have if your computer dies.
- How to use your computer and phone to remember everything you need to remember.
- How to plan things you want to do.
- Where to keep the things you always want to remember and have access to.

We will go over.
- Google docs
- Evernote
- One note
- Pocket
- Microsoft To Do
- One tab
- Google calendar
- Box
- Dropbox
- OneDrive
- I drive.
- Mega
- Carbonite

- We will also go over some computer terms you hear, but you do not know what they are.
- How to blog

- How to create quick free websites for sharing information with anyone you want.
- How to use email.
- Mind mapping to organize your thoughts for any type of project.

There are a lot of useful and productive things you can do on the internet. There are also many interesting and fun things you can do. The problem is there is a learning curve to most. This book will get you started and make it so you can use each of the items talked about to make your life easier and better. This is not a full guide to each of these things. This is for people who do not use these sites, or not much, and want to learn how.

Many of the things we will go over will be useful for most people.
Like I said, this is not a comprehensive guide to teach you all about the things in this book. This book is for people who want to learn how to use these things and save yourself time and make your life more organized.

Give it a read.

EMAIL

Social media and texting have taken over much of the daily communication people use now. Even though this is true, email is still an especially important means of communication between individuals and businesses.

Depending on who you use for your main email provider, different email programs are better than others. The biggest and most used is Outlook. I use it most of the time for my email. One reason Outlook is so popular and useful is because you can do so much with it.

You can tie other email accounts into outlook. I use it for my msn email, for my Gmail, and for my personal website email addresses. You can have several accounts on it. You can use it with POP or IMAP email accounts. Many other top programs do not work with both.

The top email programs are:

- Outlook
- Gmail

- Yahoo
- Zoho
- Yandex
- Mail

There are many others. Most of the other email services can be brought into outlook so you can see them without going to the individual web pages to access your email.

OUTLOOK

Outlook is by far my favorite and the best email program there is. The main reason I like it best is because you can access all your email accounts from the same program. It also has a good calendar, and you can set up a task list in your calendar for daily use. You can flag an email to make it a task. You can also add tasks to the list from the task list by picking new.

I put my task list for the day in my calendar so I can see it and access it from anywhere. I add my tasks at the beginning of the day, from midnight on. I put my tasks here because I do not have anything scheduled at that time of day. No space is used where I would have appointments or have other things scheduled, and I can see it all in the same place.

You can also get directly into Microsoft to do from here. I normally keep to do open all the time In one of my tabs because I use it so much.

The mobile version also gives you access to files in Google Drive, OneDrive, drop box, and box. You can also access several other things. I have Comcast home phone service, when I get a message left on the voicemail, it sends me an email with the voicemail. I can even listen to it through outlook.

I have 4 main email addresses. I have them set up, so they all come to my outlook app. I can see my main email, my Gmail, and the 2 emails I have from my website for people to reach me from there.

To set it up, just tap on the three horizontal bars at the upper left of screen. Go down to the settings and set up the different email accounts you want to access. You can just click the three bars and go to the email account you want to see.

This program has so much it can do, it makes it easy to keep track of things you need to do and what is going on that you want to keep track of.

GMAIL

Gmail is the most popular email there is, at least in the United States. I use Outlook to access my Gmail account most of the time. It is just easier because it is all together with my other emails. I do sometimes access it through the Gmail app on the computer, but rarely.

Google has a nice interface for accessing Gmail. It works well and looks nice. You can have it set up to bring in the emails into different folders. I do not like that; I like all the emails in the Inbox. It is a personal thing. Many people must like the different inboxes. There is no problem with using it. I do not use it much because it is easier to access it through Outlook.

THE WEB BROWSER

Going forward into the future, the web browser is where pretty much everything will happen on the computer. Most programs and shopping and communication, and most work, will all happen in your web browser.

What web browser you use will be determined by your personal preference. It will also depend on your work and what browser the software was written for. It will also depend on what online programs you use. Some programs work better in certain browsers.

Internet explorer is a Microsoft program, for many years they maintained control of all the development of programs to use with the browser. Chrome was open for all developers to use and create programs to work with it. This advanced Chrome right past Internet Explorer.

Because of all the development, Chrome is a more usable browser for many things. Google owns chrome. Because of that Google takes a lot of information from your searches and uses it to advertise for the companies that pay Google big money for targeted advertising.

Read about the different browsers and see what you think.

CHROME BROWSER

One of the huge things that makes Chrome the most popular and the best browser you can use, is it is what runs the Chromebook computers. Chromebooks are a great choice for many people for choosing a computer. I am writing this on a Chromebook. Because it is being used as the operating system, it must be able to do many tasks well.

I have a desktop computer, a windows laptop, and two chrome books I use. I have the desktop in my office, the windows laptop in the family room and the chrome books I take with me. I have an 11 inch one I take when I need a compact, otherwise I have a 14" one I use most of the time. I also write on a Samsung tab A tablet in Google docs. I am using it now to write this.

I do most of my writing in Google Docs. I prefer it even though I have Word, and Scrivener. I can do the same things in Docs and I can start and stop on any computer and pick up where I left off. If you are interested in writing yourself, **check out my book** on how to write and publish your own books on Amazon.

A Chromebook is a great choice for many people to access all they need to do on the internet. They are low cost, work well, and are much safer against viruses and worms than Windows based computers. I do use windows as well. Not saying it is bad.

Back to the browser
There are many reasons I use Chrome almost all the time.
- Extensions
- Safety
- Ease of use
- Add on

The extensions and add-ons are huge for me. I use Evernote in my writing and for personal use. The web clipper for Evernote is an invaluable tool for me. There are hundreds of add on and extensions you can use to make things in your everyday life much easier and more rewarding. You will need to see what is available and find out what extensions will work best for you.

To access all the extensions available in Chrome, go to the three vertical dots in the far upper right corner of the browser, just below the x. Click on the dots and go down to more tools. In the more tools drop down select extensions and find ones that will help you with things you want to do.

There is an extension called Fire shot that I use a lot. It lets you capture your screen, or parts of your screen and save them. This is a useful extension for many things. Check it out.

FIREFOX

Firefox browser used to be my favorite browser. It was the best before Chrome, then it dropped off. It has come back. Firefox is fast, and it boasts it is more private. It will bring most of your bookmarks over from Chrome. Most things you do on Chrome you can do on Firefox. It even uses one tab, which I use all the time on Chrome.

Firefox does a lot of things well. PC Magazine also voted it as the best choice browser. I have no issues with it, I like Chrome better. They say Firefox is faster, I cannot tell the difference for what I use it for. When they do the tests and measure in ms. it may be but I see no difference.

I would try to see which one you prefer.

MICROSOFT EDGE

The newest version has had the name changed to Microsoft Edge. It is fast, but it is a stripped-down bare bones browser.

I saw a cartoon that showed a picture of a figure that was internet explorer. It was looking up at a guy and asking, what am I here for? The guy looked back at the figure and said, you are here to download Chrome.

It was kind of funny, but it is the reason I have not used internet explorer for the last ten years other than at work. I used Firefox after I stopped using Internet Explorer, but when Chrome came along, I found it far superior.

Internet Explorer comes on all windows computers. It is part of windows. It is not a bad browser; it does not have the tools I like and the tools that make Chrome work better for most people.

The extensions in Chrome make it so much more useful. Internet Explorer still does not have many extensions. Because Chrome was open for developers to create extensions, everyone was making the tools for the browser that they needed to use. Microsoft was left behind because it was not open to other developers.

If you want to check email in a web browser and just general searches, Internet Explorer will work simply fine. It has gotten better and faster than it used to be. If you want to do many of the things in this book, you cannot use Internet Explorer for a lot.

Microsoft is working to catch up with Chrome, I do not know if they ever will. The lack of extensions is the biggest thing holding them back now.

Try it and see what you think. It will do a lot of what you need.

GOOGLE DOCS OVERVIEW

You can create any new document in Google Docs. A word processing document, a spreadsheet, a presentation, website, etc. This is the best thing to do if you are starting from scratch.

Creating a new document can be done from a blank document or from a template. There are many useful templates in the system for common document.

One of the cool advantages of using Google Docs is you can import many other types of documents into Google Docs and the system will convert them for you to use in Google Docs.

- Google Docs will open and convert a file while it will also store the original formatted copy for you.
- It supports .doc, .docx, .dot, .html, plain text (.txt), .odt, and .rtf.
- You can also open spreadsheets and pdf files.
- One of the coolest things is opening a PDF and converting it to a word type document you can edit and use without the PDF formatting.

- You can also create documents in Docs and save them as PDF files or excel sheets or as a doc file Microsoft Office can read.
- You can also share and collaborate the files with others to make working on group projects much easier.
- You can open the explore option and search the web and other documents you have while in the Docs page. This makes doing research in the program much easier and a more efficient use of your time.
- You can use the system offline, so you can work without an internet connection. As soon as you get an internet connection again, the system will update your files on the Google server and make it accessible everywhere you want to get it. This is a huge advantage over Microsoft programs and other writing programs. You do not have to save your copy and transfer it to the other device you were working on. With Google docs it updates to the cloud by itself and you can work on it on any device.
- You can create your own templates for documents you use.
- You can have the system create an outline on the side of the document so you can move from place to place in longer documents with ease.
- You can translate your documents into other languages with Google Translator that works with the program.

- You can switch to previous versions of your file without saving multiple copies.
- You can add images, flowcharts, spreadsheets, and any other file you want.
- You can even type by talking without other software.
- You can use add on that will help make many tasks easier and work inside the program.
- You never have to hit save. Everything you do saves as you change it.

As you can see, this program is useful and easy to use. Google makes it, and they keep adding to it all the time. It is also free to use. There are some add on you can pay for, but the overall program has not cost.

Here is a link to the Google Docs learning site if you need to get more detailed instructions on the different options.

WORD PROCESSING

There are many words processing programs available. I have tried most. I use Google docs because I have tried the others and like Google Docs best. I have taken ideas from the other programs and use them in Google Docs. It is also free for more storage than you could use.

I have used several programs to write in. I started with Microsoft word. I tried Scrivener and Google Docs. I now do all my writing in Google docs. Any program that works for you, and you like is fine. Here is why I like Google Docs.

Word works well. It has all the formatting and everything you need for writing. The downside of Microsoft Word is the limits on where you can use it. You need to do it online, or you need to have a windows computer with Word on it. If right for you, Word is an excellent option.

Many writers rave about Scrivener. It is a nice program, and once you learn how to use the features, it works well. It is again limited to how and where you can use it. If you write on one computer all the time, it is a good option. I learned great ideas from using it. Many of the ideas I use in Google Docs, I learned while working in scrivener.

The reason I now use Google Docs is that I write on three or more different computers. I have one in my office, one in my family room and a Chromebook that I take with me when I go out. Google Docs can work on the Chromebook on or offline. It also works in Windows on Chrome either online or offline. As soon as you get back online, it updates to the cloud. The program also saves all changes as soon as you make them when you are writing. If I am writing offline, I also save a copy on a flash drive, so I do not have it only on the Chromebook.

If I write on the laptop in my family room, everything I do is on the cloud. If I write on my desktop in the office, everything is on the cloud right away. I can switch from the family room to the office or vice versa, and I do not have to take a copy on a flash drive. It is all updated everywhere right away. We have a cabin where we spend a lot of time during the summer; the Chromebook and my Samsung tablet are perfect for that.

There is no Internet there. Because of the long battery life of the Chromebook, I can write for 8 to 10 hours without plugging in. That is another huge advantage of using the Chromebook. At the cabin, I save it on the computer and on the flash drive just in case it is lost.

I also turn on the hotspot on my phone, which does work at the cabin, and it updates my writing. If I do not update it over the hotspot, when I get home, it updates to the cloud, and I can access it anywhere again.

Google Docs now has several other things I use that are very handy. There is voice typing option you can use to talk, and the program converts it to text. I have used Dragon software for this in the past, and Google does a more accurate job of converting it to text. I do not use it this way a lot, but it is nice sometimes.

Another thing I use for editing is an add on called Pro Writing Aid. It has a small cost to get it, but it is valuable when editing. You can check grammar. You can also check writing style and several other things. This will tighten up you are writing and make it the best it can be.

You can also have an outline set up on the left side of the screen while you are writing. It is easy to get to the part of your book you want to go to by picking where you want to go from the outline. On the right side, you can research without leaving the document writing screen. This is one thing Scrivener has that I liked.

Another part of Scrivener I liked is you can have each chapter separated while writing. Breaking the book into pieces makes it simpler and less overwhelming when you do the rewriting and editing. Looking at 2 to 10 pages feels much easier than looking at 100 pages.

I do this in Google docs. I make a document for each chapter and section of the book. I write in those documents. When the main writing is done, I re write and edit in the separate documents. Then when it is ready, I put it all together in the right order in a main document.

You can do any word processing work on Google Docs. You can save it right in the program. You can access it anywhere.

SPREADSHEETS

If you are familiar with spreadsheets, this one works the same as most. I was used to Microsoft Excel and could use Google Docs right away.

There are features that Excel has that Google docs does not, but most things you will use a spreadsheet for in non-business use, this program will do for you.

Spreadsheets are great for sorting and manipulating data to give you results you want to track and use. They are also great for storing information in tables where you want to keep things organized and separated.

Here are things I use them for that are non-business related.

- Comparisons if you are looking to make larger purchases. List the features and the pros and cons of each item so you can compare them side by side.
- Tracking lists, like information about people. You can have each member of your family in a column. In the rows you can put things like

favorite things, what they like, gift ideas, birthdays, etc.

- Keeping track of running totals on things. Expenses. Where you spend money.
- Things you want to sort. You can sort by date, alphabetic, a bigger number, etc.
- Any list where you want to do a mathematical operation with a date. Averages, totals, etc.
- Any financial tracking.
- Donations to charities.
- You can track things you use and rate them. Beer, wine, etc.
- Workout reps and weights.
- Keep track of music you have.
- Track movies you watch and what you think of them.
- Health data. Blood pressure, sugar readings for diabetics, etc.
- The possibilities are endless for what you can track.
- There are templates available that will let you do many of these things that are already created for your use.
- You can also create graphs from the data in your spreadsheets.

They are easy to use to do most things you will want to do with a spreadsheet. Experiment with it and see all the things you can do.

- Go to Google Drive and select new.
- Select Google sheets. Move your mouse over to the right where the arrow is and select a template. Look to see if there is a template that will do what you want to do first. If not, you can choose blank, but look first for a template.
- You can edit the templates to do most of the things you want. Select something that does the thing you want to use the sheet for.
- If there are not templates you feel you can make work, use a blank one and make your own. Open a template first to see things you can do with them.

As an example:
You can use the assignment tracker to store things like movies you watch.
You can change the headings of the columns to store the info you want.
Change the assignment tracker header to movie tracker.
You can change the text in the text box to the right to whatever you want to say, or just delete it.

- Column 1 can be the type of movie. Action, suspense, kids, etc.
- Column 2 the title of the movie.
- Column 3 can be how you rate it.
- Column 4 can be the rating of the movie, G, PG, R, etc.
- Column 5 can be run-time.
- Column 6 can be date you watched it.

You can adjust the width of the columns at the top by just moving the borders.
You can add more columns and add more rows.
You can use different fonts and different colors.
You can add links to web pages like the review on rotten tomatoes for the movie.
You can search and find a movie by title, or by any other column you have in your sheet. The possibilities are unlimited for what you can store and track.

Spreadsheets are useful for many things. Use them to make your life easier and more organized.

CREATE A WEBSITE

Having your own website is fun for a lot of different things. There are hundreds of sites you can go to for creating a website, many of them are free. If you are using it for a business or for making money, do not use a free site. It does not look professional. For business you need to at least have your own domain of your business.

If you want to create a fun site for personal or family use, the best and easiest site is Google sites. It is part of the Google group of programs. You can access it from the Google docs. It is by far the easiest site to create a website.

Here is how to set up your own website.

The first thing to do is to lay out what you want the site to look like.
You can do this on a piece of paper. You have a home page. That is the main page that your site will open to. This is a great place to use a mind map to lay out your website before you start building it. All you do then is add the pieces and put it together.

Decide what pages you want on your website.

- An About me page. Tells about you and why you made the site.
- A contact pages. This can be part of the about me page. Any contact info you want to share. Email is the best way.
- Then add other pages. As an example, if you want to set up a site for your photos. You can have a page for friends, travel, animals, family, etc. whatever you want to show on separate pages. If you want to make a site to share family news and communicate with others in the family. You can set up a page for each family, or each person in the family. You can have a page about what they are doing, pictures to show what they are doing, etc. The only limit to what you can create is your imagination and who you want to share it with.
- Decide who you want to share the page with. Do you want it for family only? Do you want the page to be public so anyone can see it?

SETTING UP YOUR SITE

- Open Google Drive
- Click on new.
- Go down to more.

- Click on Google sites. This will open a blank site to build on.
- On the top row, there is a picture of a person with a + next to it. If you want to allow others to edit the page, you can give them access here. This is nice if you want to do a family site and allow a member from each family to update their family news. Others in the family can all update their pages, and everyone will keep up on all the family news.
- Next pick a theme. Check out the different ones to see what you like best.
- You have a few font choices and colors you can use.
- Put the cursor over the page title and give your site a title. My family, or whatever you want.
- Move your mouse over the header and pick the header type.
- Go to the pages tab and click on that.
- Click on the + button so you can add pages.
- When you get to this point, you can publish. The first time you publish you have a couple other things to do. Type in what you want to call the site. Until you find a name available. You can also click in the box to not have search engines index the site. This means that only people you give the site address will

access the site. If you want it public, do not click in the box.

- Click on publish. At the bottom of the screen, you can view what it looks like on the internet. Close that view and go back to the editor when you have looked it over. It is not that impressive yet, but you have a good start.
- Click on each page at the top to go to that page. Set the header type for each page. You can change the header to a picture or a design. Click on the change image in the header. You can pick from some that they have for you. You can upload a picture from your computer, or you can access photos in your Google photos albums. You can experiment with these until you get the look you want.
- Next you can go to the Home page and set up what you want the homepage to say and to show. This is the main page people will see when they come to the site. Decide what you want to be here.
- Click on the insert tab on the upper right of the screen to add content.
- You can add pictures, YouTube videos, you can add text boxes to type in anything you want. You can add a link to pictures and text.

You can make lists with links. You can use files and charts, just about anything.

- Every item you add will have a box pop up on the top where you can create a link or change other attributes. On the far left there is another box that will let you change the background of the object.
- You can do just about anything and create a site to share anything you want to with a little work, and it works well.

Just hit the publish button anytime you change something, and it goes live on the internet. After you publish the site, go to the home page, and copy that web address. That is the address you want to give to the people you want to share the site with.

It will save the website in your Google Drive, so accessing it to change the site is easy and fun. This is not for a business or a site you want to make money on the internet, but if you are reading this book, that is not likely your goal. This is for personal use you want to do for free and you need no experience to set up. It makes a functional and nice website.

Here is a book website I created with this method to get people to my books. It only took me a short time, and it is functional and effective. It also looks good on a mobile device.

As far as I know, there is no limit on the number of websites you can create. So have fun and create websites for whatever you want to share.

PRESENTATIONS

The presentations that you can do in Google Docs are limited. If you are a user of PowerPoint, this is not for you. It is not PowerPoint and not for business presentations.

If you want to make a simple presentation for showing someone a group of pictures, or other simple things that you can go through and display, it will do some easy ones.

Go to Google Drive:
- Click on New and mouse down to Google Slides.
- Mouse to the right and select from a template.
- Pick one that you think you can edit to fit what you want to do with it.
- If there is not one you think will work, pick blank. Use a template if you can, it will make it easier.

Example:
If you want to take a photo presentation, choose Yearbook.
- Change the title to what you want.

- Right click on a picture and go down to replace image and insert the picture you want to use.
- Fill in the slides that are there. You can right click on the slides on the left side and duplicate them or change them to look like you want.
- You can add text boxes and put text anywhere you want on the slides.
- In the row above you can make other changes to create the slideshow you want.
- Pick the transition you want to use between slides.
- Click on the presentation square at the top right side and click present from beginning and watch the slideshow.
- Go back in and edit what you feel would be better.
- You can add on extra things here.
- There is an add on that will let you add audio files to your presentations. This makes them much more useful. You need to have the audio files in your Google Drive for the add on to pull them up for you.
- Keep watching and working on the slide show until you get it to where you want it to be.

- You can download the file as a PowerPoint file that will play on almost any computer.
- If you show the slideshow in Google Drive, there is a pointer you can use with your mouse to highlight things in the show.

PIXLR PHOTO EDITOR

Pixlr is a capable photo editor that will allow you to do most of the things you want to do with your photos. It can do most of the things you want to do with other photo editing programs. The big difference is the cost. It is free to use. If you know anything about photo editing, you will figure it out easily.

Go to new in Google docs and move down to more. Click on Pixlr editor and open the program. Select start a new photo or upload one from your computer.

To learn more about the program, click on the help tab at the top and learn all you need to know about using the program.

If you want to edit photos on your phone, check out my book and taking great photos with a phone camera.

ADD ONS

There are some add on you can add to Google docs. A few of them are free. There is one I use and love. It is called Pro Writing Aid. If you are a writer, it is fantastic.

If you are a writer check it out. What it does is gives you several reports you can run that will check your grammar, style, overused words, consistency, acronyms, sticky sentences, and several others. You can then edit the entire document with the program. It will give you suggestions on how to edit it to make it easier to read and more effective. It is a useful add on for Google docs.

There is a highlighting tool that can be useful. Especially if you share and collaborate with others. It is also good for proofreading when you find mistakes or things you want to change.

There is a couple hundred add on you can add. Some are free, some cost money. Go to the add on header, go to the bottom, and click on get add on. It will take you to the Google page to get add on. There are many good ones. Look for add on that will help you do the things you use Google Docs for that will make it easier and better for what you are doing.

STORING AND ORGANIZING

There are several programs I use for storage and organizing. Some work better for some things, others work better for other things. Here are the ones I use, what I use them for and how to use them. They are all free to use. Some of them have a paid version as well. There is only one I used the paid version for, Evernote. I use it for more than I can with the free version.

The free version is very usable for what most people want to use it for. I use Evernote for my book research, and I save a lot of websites on different subjects to review for later. I have over 15,000 notes in Evernote and it will continue to grow for a long time. I have my own internet of things I am interested in with Evernote. and I can access it offline, anywhere I need to access it, and from any device.

Most of these programs allow you to share your pages, and folders as well. This gives you the ability to share what you have and let others add and change things so others can collaborate on what you are doing.

HERE ARE THE ONES I USE
- Evernote
- Google Docs
- OneNote
- Wunderlist
- One drive
- Pocket

There are more good storage places on the web. These are easy to use and they work well.

EVERNOTE

Evernote is my favorite and most useful program for saving and organizing things I do and want to save for the future. Web pages or articles from the internet. There are many books about Evernote that show you how to use it. They all have good ideas in them. I will give you the best ideas I have found and the best practices for ease of use.

There are several versions of Evernote. I use all on different devices. Go to evernote.com to sign up for an account. There is a desktop version, a web version and mobile versions for Android and Apple. There is also a web clipper vital to getting the most out of the program. Install the web clipper in the extensions in Chrome.

Using Evernote is free for most of what you want it for. You can store a huge amount of data in the system for free. You are limited on how much you can save into Evernote with the free option. It is more than most people will need.

DESKTOP VERSION

This is my main version. It is the best and easiest to work with. This one you download to your computer and it runs on your system.

- Create a notebook for things you want to save. Create more notebooks for main things you want to save. Create notebooks like, places I want to see, things I want to do, books to read, things you want to remember. You can make notebooks for hobbies and sports. Workouts. Take pictures of receipts to save, save them together with others for the same things.
- Anything you are interested in saving for future use. Contact lists for friends, business contacts, family birthdays and anniversaries, other useful information. There is really no limit to what you can save.

When you get what you think are the main notebooks you want to save. You can group notebooks into similar groups such as receipt. Inside receipts you can have, food, clothing, gas, etc. in what is called stacks.

Hold the mouse on one type of receipt and move it on top of another of your notebooks. It will group them into what is called a stack. Right click on where it says notebook stack and rename it to receipts stack. You will have all your categories of receipts in a stack for receipts. Evernote puts your notes in Alphabetical order. You can add a prefix to make them be higher on the page.! is the top, the @ is next.! @ would be at the top of the list.

Have your main listed as! main or! master stack to keep it at the top. Keep all your main notebooks here. The ones you will use often. You can store anything in Evernote. Files, web pages, pictures, pdfs, videos, etc. anything you need to save. When you start, keep things organized, this does not seem necessary at first. When you get to where you have thousands of notes, and hundreds of notebooks you will be glad you did.

As you save things in Evernote, add tags to what you save, and store them in different notebooks so they are easier to find. You can search by any words. The program will find the word in any document you have saved. Tags make it much more selective when you search.

The search capability of Evernote makes it awesome when you get lots of notes. You can search by a word or a phrase and it will pull up all the places it shows up in your notes.

For example, I am a fishing fanatic, mostly bass. I have thousands of articles saved about fishing. I can type in the search bar spinnerbaits in weeds. It will pull up all the articles and highlight the phrase in every one of them.

As you save things in Evernote, keep creating new notebooks and stacks to store your things in. Tags are not needed, but they make it easier to search when you want to pull things back up. It is easy to find things for a while. When you get to where you have thousands of notes and articles saved, it gets harder, so tagging is desirable.

When you save things using the clipper, most of the saved items will be easier to read and better to find if you save them as a simplified article. If you save it like that, it takes off all the ads and garbage off the page, so it only saves what you want. You can choose what you save. Most of the time the simplified is the best.

You can also create templates to use with evernote. There are premade templates you can download and use in your notes. Here is a list of some of the good ones and the instructions on how to use them.

Set up your most used and favorite notebooks as shortcuts. The shortcuts show up on the top bar of the program so you can get to them anytime right away. They also show up quickly and easily in all access to Evernote. The mobile and web versions.

Templates are also easy to make on your own. The best thing to do is to set up a template notebook. Set it up as a shortcut so it is easy to get to when you need it.

To create a template, make a note and add all the things to the note you want. You can take some premade ones you can download and change them to what you need them to do.

You can also start from scratch. Open a new note in the template notebook and add anything you want. Everything is available. Tables are very handy for templates. You can add pictures, other files, text, tables, anything you need.

When you finish the template, right click on it, and click on the copy to a notebook. Pick the notebook you want to copy it to, and you are ready to use it. Do not change the template. Leave it in the template notebook for further use. When you want to use it as a template, go to the template notebook and copy it to the notebook you want to save it in, and you are ready to go.

Here is an example of a different template I use. I wanted to have a template I can use every day to keep track of things, and to make sure I write every day. I call it my daily journal. I set up this simple note I copy to my Journal notebook every day and enter the info I want.

I have a title at the top. The next part is happening today. In this section I put what I am doing, and things happening in the world today. The next section is a picture of the day. Most of them are pictures I take. If I do not have a picture I want to add, I find one online that is cool. I put it there for something to remember, or something to take one as good myself. The last section is daily writing. I want to make sure I write something every day. This is above and beyond working on my books. This can be anything from answering a question to writing my feelings on something in the news that day.

Here is an example of the blank template I use. I fill it in every day. I have a journal notebook in a Journaling stack. I have a notebook for each month with a note for each day of the month. The title of each note is that days date. I can find out what I did on any day I want. See my photo of the day and see what I wrote that day.

The great thing about doing it like this is that the format is always the same and I can search them if I need to. Every note is a different length, and that's ok because Evernote stores it all. This was my original template. I have changed it several time since and added and taken away from it. I now have it to save everything I want each day.

MY DAILY JOURNAL

HAPPENING TODAY

You can create templates for anything you do. There are good ones you can download for meetings, budgets, and tracking anything you want. If you are a student, you can have a class note template you can use to take your notes and track what you did in each class that day. Have a notebook for each class. You can have the title of the notes as a date or you can have it as the subject of the lecture. Whatever you want to see to find your notes.

You can tag each one so you can search and find what you are looking for. And you can have it all with you all the time on your phone, tablet, or laptop. You can also set up to have access to notebooks offline. This makes it perfect for a small light and inexpensive Chromebook that you do not even need an internet connection to take notes. As soon as you get online after your done working, it syncs, and you now have all your work on every device.

I use Evernote on my Desktop, my windows laptop, 2 Chromebooks, a Samsung galaxy tab A, 2 kindle fires and my cell phone. You can also use the microphone option on your computer or phone, or tablet and you do not even need to type. You can talk at a steady pace and let the computer type it for you.

You can also save audio recordings, video recordings, photos from anywhere. You can also copy files from Google Drive into Evernote. Open Google Drive and open the file you want to copy. Click on the Google Drive symbol to add and copy it into evernote. You can even search your files in Google docs to find what you want.

You can also add files from anywhere on your computer, or any other computer you can access. You can use this to transfer files from one computer to another if you need it on that computer.

The program is so versatile and so useful for so many things. You need to check it out. The free version will do most thing for most people.

MICROSOFT TO DO

There is a lot of good to do list programs available. Wunderlist is the best I have found. What makes it so good is you can store and organize lists like the other programs. The best thing you can do is have lists inside lists, with notes. The free version is exceptionally good.

You can also email you or someone else a copy of your lists and what you have saved. You can print a copy. You can create another copy; you can share it with someone else.

Open the program.
- In the lower left of screen, click create list.
- Give it a name. I make my main names in all caps. Not something you have to do.
- Click in the add a to do and type something you want a list for. These need not be to do lists. You can make them anything you want a list for. I use it for my grocery list every week. That way I can add things as I think of them throughout the week.
- After you add an item, hit enter and it puts it in the list.

- Double click on the item and it opens things you can do on the right side. You can set a date when you want to have it done. You can set a reminder, so you do not forget.
- You can add subtasks. This works good for storing things other than to do lists. For example, if you want a list to store passwords. You can set up a list of passwords. In the list you can create an item for each type of passwords. Example would be work passwords, website passwords, phone passwords, etc. As many as you want to keep them organized.
- You can change a list or item by double clicking it and change it. You can also just click in the box and delete it and make a new one.
- In the work password item, double click and select add a subtask. Add what the subtask is and the password for it. Create as many subtasks as you need for your list. If you want to add any notes to the item in the list, you can do that.
- You can also attach a file if you need to.
- You can also move your lists into groups of lists. Example. You can create a do today list. A do this week list. A do this month list. You can then move them and put them into a

group that you can name to do lists. You can open and close the group to see what is in it.
- You can drag and move lists or groups to have them in an order you want. The program is especially useful for many things. Anything you want to have in a list or a group of lists, wunderlist is the best program.

Experiment with the program and you will find all kinds of things you can use to make life easier and more organized.

GOOGLE DOCS

You can also use Google Docs to store any
document and pictures you want to save for use
later.

To use for storage, go to Google Drive and make
sure you are in my drive. Click on new. From that
new button select new folder. Give the folder a
name you want to use to store the files you want to
store.

Click on the folder you created in the Google Drive
and click on new.
Click on file upload or folder upload and select what
you want to take from your computer to Google
Docs.

You can do this with anything you want to save.
Your stuff will be stored where it will be safe.

I have a separate chapter on Google docs, check it
out.

ONENOTE

OneNote is a Microsoft product that comes with Office. It also comes free without Office. It has great potential as being useful. The latest version that comes with Windows 10 is much better than previous versions. This program is great for storing things you want to save for easy access. If you are wanting to save web pages or other internet things, Evernote is much better.

The older versions are not as easy to figure out the steps to use it and how to best make it work for you. I would not even try if you do not know how to use it. If you have the newer version, you can try it.

The biggest problems I have with the new version is it is extremely hard to delete a notebook. You can close them, so they are not on your main page. To delete it, go to the file viewer and find the folder for OneNote and find the notebook and delete it.

If you want to try it, it works well for storing things you want to keep and remember.
Open the program and create a notebook that will be your main storage notebook. To create a

notebook, click on the +notebook at the bottom of the column.

As an example. If you want to store tax forms. Create a notebook called My forms. Go to the sections, delete the new Section 1 section. Create a section tax forms. Then create a page for my tax forms, tax forms, business tax forms, kids tax forms, etc.

You can copy and paste, add them as images, anything you want you can save here. You can add a new section for mortgage papers, other loan papers, any forms you want to keep track of you can save under the forms section.

You can create other notebooks and other sections and other pages depending on what you want to store. You can store pictures, lists of links you like to go to, you can store an inventory of your house with pictures and descriptions. There is no end to the things you can store.

There is also a web clipper you can use to save web pages you want to keep the info for later, or you want to read later. To use the web clipper, install the extension. I use Chrome. Then when you want to save a page, click on the icon on the top of your screen and it will ask you were to save it. Save it for later.

It is also good for students to take notes and keep them organized for study and for review. You can have a notebook for each class. Have a section for each type of thing for a class such as quizzes, notes, handouts, tests, etc. you can keep everything sorted for future use.

Home inventory is another great task for OneNote. Create a notebook for home inventory. Create a section for each room you want to record your belongings. Then in each room you can set up a page for types of things or put them all in a single page. You should create a page that shows the item in a picture and a description of the item. If you have receipts or a manual, you can take a picture of that to show model number etc.

You can use it to go all digital with your important papers, save your receipts and everything else you need to save.

The one huge bonus over using paper notebooks is, you can add in new notes or ideas, you can add pictures, you can highlight notes, you can add tables, you can draw pictures. Anything that will make your notes better and easier to study can be added wherever you want to add it. It also stores the info on the cloud, so it will not get lost or damaged in a fire or other disaster.

I use the program for storing files I want to save I need not access regularly. Files like tax files and other forms I want to be able access when I need to, but not on all my devices. It does not sync well all the time. Once it syncs, it has the information on each device.

It is a useful product for the right things. I would use Evernote for most things you want to store. Evernote it is a much better program. If you do not have the newest version of OneNote, I would not use it, it is too difficult to get around in. You can download the newest version for free. **Here is where to get OneNote.**

There is an online version as well that you can use.
The online version is harder to delete notebooks.

Here is the Microsoft help page if you have problems with using the program.

ONE DRIVE

I use OneDrive for a couple of reasons.

- It works best for saving Microsoft files to be used on different devices.
- It also works well for sharing or accessing large files that are too big to email. This is the main benefit of one drive. Some files are too big to email, one drive can overcome that issue by sharing the files on OneDrive that are too big to email.

They have different plans you can get. I use the free plan. It gives you 5gb of storage. If you want more, you can buy a paid plan. The paid plans are not expensive if you need the extra space.

POCKET

Pocket is the program I use for saving videos I want to share or go back and watch again later. I store videos like fishing techniques on how to do different things to improve my fishing.

I store other videos I see I want to watch later.

The best way to use it is to set up an account.

Set up the web clipper in Chrome so you can save what you want.

- Go to extensions in the Chrome browser.
- Set up the pocket clipper.
- Go to YouTube and when you find videos you want to save.
- Click on the clipper in the bar of the browser.
- Add a tag to the page as you save it so you can search for it later.
- When you want to watch the videos go to pocket and pick your video

You can store other things here on Pocket. I only use it for videos, so they are all in one place when I want to see them.

SEARCHING THE INTERNET

GOOGLE

How to search Google

- You can go to Google and type in the word or phrase you are looking for and most of the time find what you want.
- If you want to narrow the search. Put quotes around your search. This will search for the exact phrase in the quotes.
- Use an * inside the quotes to look for an unknown variable. Ex. "* the bell tolls" It will pull up all the references to for whom the bell tolls and anything else that fits that exact phrase.
- To search a specific website, type in for example. Wikipedia site: disc golf. This will show you all the mentions of disc golf on Wikipedia.
- You can search over 100 years of newspaper articles on a subject at this <u>Google search site.</u>

- You can do comparison searches by using vs. Example. type "green beans vs. peas". Do not forget the quotes.
- You can get the meaning of words by typing define and the word. Example. Define middle age.
- You can type Related: anything. It will bring up sites related to what you typed. Example related: walmart.com. It will pull up sites like Walmart. It will also give you more info about things at Walmart. Try a search like this and by just typing in Walmart and you will see the difference. It is a good way to get more specific information on a subject.
- If you are trying to see what something looks like. Type it in, then click on images. Example, banana spider. Do not use these images unless you do an advanced search and find ones that are usable. Most are not. But it is a quick way to see what something looks like.
- You can type in burgers nearby and you will get a list and map of burger places close to your location.
- You can type flip a coin and it will randomly flip a coin for you.
- You can type temperature in wherever you want, and Google will tell you.

- You can type in weather for wherever you want to know, and it will give it to you.
- You can type in math problems for an answer.
- You can type in many questions. How many cm in an inch?
- How far is it to wherever you want to go? It will use your current location and tell you how far. You can also ask from point to point.
- You can also hit the microphone on the search bar and search by asking instead of typing.

As you type into Google, it thinks ahead to find what you are trying to find out. Use the drop-down list to save typing and get your answer faster.

You can experiment and see what else you can find. If you use all the capabilities of Google, you can find out most things you want to know and quick.

KINDLE BOOKS

If you are a reader and you want to have access to millions of books, Kindle is the place to be. You can read almost any book you want on a Kindle. You can find hundreds of books to read for free on kindle. There are many ways to find them. I wrote a whole book about it.

You can go to Amazon and search for free books and find many. If you want to see all the best ways to find free books for kindle, **check out my book.**

Here is the intro to the book.

Almost everyone reads. Many people read lots of books, or you read online articles. Many people read news stories, or blogs. Almost everyone reads several or all the above.

What this book will do is show you the best places to find the books you enjoy reading. It will also show you where to get most for free.

How you read has changed a lot over the past few years. There are many people who still read paper books. The trend is changing, and more people do most of their reading on electronic media. Where you read now ranges from computers, phones, laptops, and tablets.

Some types of media are better than others for reading because of ease of use. Phones are small and are difficult to read books on. Computers are big, somewhat bulky, and you must sit at a desk. Laptops are much the same; you are stuck sitting at a table or desk.

So, when most people want to enjoy reading, they choose a tablet or e reader type device. The favorite type of device is a version of a Kindle.

If you have an Amazon account, you can download the books free. Then using the Kindle, or using the Kindle app, you can read the book on the device you choose. There are a few reasons I prefer using the actual Kindle device itself. The Kindle HDX, the fire 8 and the fire 10 will read almost any books I download. I can do other things while listening to the books I want.

Other Kindle devices do not have the read to you option available on them. The Kindle paperwhite is an excellent choice if you want to use it for reading. The other Kindle e-readers are also great for reading books and other documents. The newer Kindle fires can read to you. It is very convenient.

I would recommend that you have a Kindle for reading your books. Like I said it is unnecessary, but it is easier, and you can turn it on in a couple of seconds.

If you do not, have a Kindle, you can download the app to a phone, or tablet. You can even read them right on your computer screen with the Kindle app.

There are millions of good books out there. Most of them are downloadable to the Kindle device or app. Most of the books listed on these sites are free, and nothing beats getting them free.

I have downloaded several thousand books over the past five years. Only about 50 of them were not free. I have access to them any time I want to read them again.

I have also purchased several books from the Amazon site. That is why Amazon can offer them free. Amazon has a great program for authors to help them promote their books for free.

When authors offer them free, they get them in the hands of more people. Amazon knows you will buy books along with the free ones. This makes it a win-win for everybody involved.

Look at what is available. Even if you do not have a device to read them, look through the books on Amazon, look at the books that are available. See the amazing amount of knowledge, and just fun reading you can get at no cost to you.

This book will show you many places to you can get free, or reasonable priced Kindle books. You can download them to any of your devices and read them whenever you want. Many sites have a sign-up where you can get an email list every day.

With your Amazon account, you get unlimited storage of the books you downloaded. All the books you download free or paid. You can go into the archives any time and download the books to any device and read it again. Or read it for the first time if you have not gotten to it yet.

As you get new devices, you can log in and get the books on those devices.

I like to get them from the emails. The emails are easy to follow up on and download them to your device. Then you can read them as soon as you want to. It is simple to do, and a cool way to get free books. As you get to each chapter, the blue title heading on the page is a link to the site in that chapter. The best places for you to get your free books.

This book will open the world of free Amazon Kindle books. There are enough new free books to keep you busy reading for years and years to come.

If you are not interested in getting this book that gives you access to all the best sites, you can go to Amazon and in the search bar, select Kindle store and search free books. This will give you a good look at what you can get for free.

If you read fiction books, most authors will give you the first book free, or at low cost to get you to read it and then buy the rest of the books in the series. This is how they sell books. It is also how you can decide if the story is worth paying for. If you buy the other books in the series, they are not expensive. It is a win win for authors and readers.

One cool thing you can do with a Kindle is read a book, take notes, and digitally save them to a computer.

Go to Amazon and get a Kindle book you want to read.
Download it to your kindle.
As you read through the book and find things you want to save to remember for later. Use a stylus and hold it on the part you want to save. This will select it. Highlight it with any color.

Go through the whole book and highlight all the parts that you want to save.

After you finish the book, tap on a part on any page where there is no text.

At the top you will see what looks like a piece of paper with writing on it. Tap on it.

It will show the places you highlighted in the book. Tap on the symbol at the upper right that looks like a sideways v. Two lines with a dot on the end of each line.

At the bottom it will show make flashcards or export notebook.

Pick export notebook.

Pick APA and export.

Select email and email the notebook to your email address.

When you get the email open it up and double click on the link in the email.

Save it as an HTML document.

Open the document as a web page.

Copy the document and save it to the program you want to save it in, and you are done.

OTHER PLACES TO SEARCH

Here are other options for you to search to find the best of what you are looking for.

Duckduckgo This is a good fast search engine. The second best for finding info fast and easy. It is remarkably like Google in what you get in your searches. The big difference is they do not track what you do and do not use your information. If that bothers you with Google, this is a great alternative. I do not have an issue with how Google works. That is their main business. They put ads for people's products on the pages that people are looking for. DuckDuckGo does something else. It does not give you pages like the others. It gives you one long page so you can just keep scrolling down.

Bing is a search engine that is run by Microsoft. I have no problem with how Bing works. I do not like the looks. I think Bing is better than Dogpile. It is likely the third best to search.

Dogpile gets its search info from other search engines like Google. They have different algorithms they feel give you better results of what you are looking for. The searches I have done to compare show me that in my opinion, Google does a better job of giving me what I am looking for.

Yippy One thing Yippy does that is kind of cool is that when you do a search, it gives you a list on the left side that drills down deeper into what you want to find. It gives you a few choices to drill down. Sometimes this is nice because it is easy to access. It is also right there at the top, and easy to access. It also gives you the number of pages on each subgroup it found. Google has a similar list on the bottom of every search page. This is right at the top. I still prefer what Google gives you on your searches. It is another option though.

Wikipedia is sometimes criticized because anyone can add info to it. Some info may not be correct, but not everything on the internet is correct, much of it is not. Wikipedia is a good source of information on many subjects. If you want a quick search about a topic, you can get a lot of great information from this site.

Yahoo is still there, and it is worth checking sometimes. It can give some different results that may be the exact thing you are looking for. It is worth checking, especially if you do not find the exact thing you are looking for on Google.

Quora This is not your normal search engine. Quora is set up to answer questions. The questions are answered by other people on the internet. It can sometimes be useful if you are looking for something specific and you cannot find your answer.

YouTube is the best search engine there is if you want to find out how to do something. Just about anything. From changing the taillight in your car, to cleaning a deer. Anything you want to see how to do you can find on YouTube.

Creative Commons This is where you can search if you are looking for photos to use on a website or in commercial advertising. Make sure you check the licensing before you use any photos, but this is a great place to find quality photos.

If you search Google and these other search engines and you cannot find what you are looking for, it does not exist.

MIND MAPPING

There are many mind mapping programs you can get. Some are better than others. You should find one you like and use it. Mind mapping is outlining and organizing your thoughts, it makes things work better and more efficiently. If you do any writing or need to organize thoughts for a meeting or even a project, mind mapping is the way to go. You can set up everything you want to talk or write about. You can get all your thoughts together in a way that makes sense.

Of all the mind mapping programs available, **Xmind is my favorite to use.** It is free, and it exports to Evernote. The only downside is the versions not in windows do not work as well. There are many other programs you can use. Google Docs even has one that is workable if you need it. It is better than some I have tried. Get one and learn to use it. There are many mind maps programs, I have not tried them all and likely never will. The main point is finding one you like and use it. It will help you a lot to organize your thoughts. If you write with a competed mind map, you will never have writer's block.

Free mind is another good program. It is also easy to use and works well with multiple browsers.

Google Docs also has a workable mind map program, but they limit it, and you must pay if you use over 3 mind maps.

Mindjet is another good mind map program that I use, and it works well. It is a great program, but they have changed it recently and it does not have a free version anymore. Like I said, there are many mind maps programs that are available. Find one you like and use it.

XMIND

XMIND

Sign up for the program and download it. Get the free version to try it out. The free version does what I need it to do. It may be all you need. There is a pro version you can pay for that adds more features.

Once you download and open the program, follow these steps to get up and running.

- Pick the type of mind map you want to create. I use the first one for most of my mind maps.
- Click on the one you want to use. Pick one you prefer.
- Type the main topic of the mind map in the center box.
- Have the box highlighted that you want to add new points and hit the tab button on the computer. It will create a new box. Enter the point in that box.
- Highlight the new box and hit the tab button and enter subheadings for that topic.
- You keep adding the topics and subtopics until you cover everything you want to cover in the article or the book. As far as I know there is no limit to the number of topics and

subtopics you can use. You rarely need to go over 2 or 3 deeps.

- Once you get everything on the mind map, you can move the order around, so you have them in the places you want them to be in your article or book or plan. Just click your mouse on the group to move and drag it to a new spot.
- When you get it, all done like you want it, you can save it to your computer, or you can save it as an image to Evernote so you can keep it available to use. Save it to your computer first, so you can always edit or add to it if needed.

Other mind map programs should work. There will be slight differences in how the programs work, but they will be similar.

This is the best way there is to organize your ideas and thoughts. Mind maps can be used for so many things you want to do.

What you can use mind maps for:
- Creating presentations
- Event planning
- Goal setting
- Articles
- Blogs

- Meetings
- Note taking for lectures.
- Note taking when reading technical books.
- Laying out a website design

And thousands of other things. Try them and make your life easier.

Here is a sample of what it looks like.

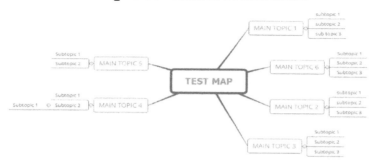

COGGLE

This mind map tool is easy to use. The learning curve on this program is about 1 minute. A good one to try. You can have 3 private mind maps and unlimited public ones. For most things this will work well for most people.

There is an app for iPhone for Coggle and android also, so you can use it on all your devices.

It needs no tutorial at all. Go to the site and use it.

FREE MIND

This program gets excellent reviews by CNET, it is one site I look at and agree with most of their reviews. **Here is the best download site**.

They give this program an excellent rating and it is free to use. I have been using xmind since it came out and I like it, so I have not used free mind but try it. Otherwise use xmind.

I have used Coggle as of late and like how easy it is to use.

KADAZA

This is one of the most useful websites you will ever use. Go to Kadaza.com and set it up. Use this as your start page. You can easily find anything on the internet you are looking for.

Set up the main page for the sites you use most. If you cannot get them all on the front page, you can access most usable sites from the other links. It is simple to set up. Nothing more to say, just use it.

Here is my home page.

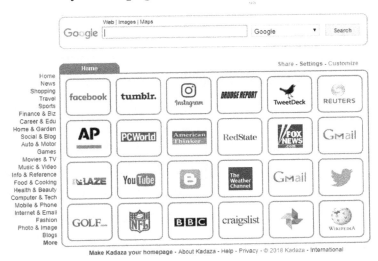

HOME NEW TAB PAGE

This is another cool extension for Chrome. Go to the Chrome web store and type in the search box Home new tab page. It will pull up the extension window that looks like this.

Click on this to install the extension and use it on Chrome. What this extension does is give you a great start-up screen every time you open a new tab on Chrome. You can customize it to show you many things on opening. Here is a look at mine.

As you can see it gives you access to apps. The plus sign on the right scrolls to more pages of apps. It gives you notifications from Google plus, Facebook etc., It shows you emails; it shows weather, time, date, you can make notes on the page to see later. It is a very handy page and a good place to start when you open the computer.

GOOGLE CALENDAR

Google calendar is a great calendar and is useful. I use the calendar more that is part of Outlook. Just because it is always there on all my devices. I use outlook for all my email, and the calendar is always right there with it.

You can set up Google calendar, so it syncs with apple calendar. You can have it show you different things you are interested in. For example, you can have it show you your favorite sports teams and when they play. It will also show you the scores after the games.

You can have it show you holidays, birthdays, and many other things. You can also have it show you tasks to do. I do not like the way the tasks part works so I do not use that. I use Wunderlist for my to do lists; it works better for me.

If you want a good calendar and you do not use Outlook, use Google Calendar. It also has a task list built into it on the upper right side to help make it even more useful.

Here is a shot of mine.

ADD TO ANY

This is another Chrome extension I use a lot. It is great for adding a web page or an article to a blog or a web sharing site. I have blogs I update with information I find on the topics I am interested in.

These blogs are full of great articles about these things. Anyone can go to them and get access to tons of information about the subjects I update. I did this many years ago, to store and have access to the information I wanted to save to read later or have access to for learning. It morphed into a great resource for anyone who wants to use it. Here is a link to my website. All the blogs are linked on my website on the pages under the subjects listed.

It also works great to add a story or article you read to many social media sites in a convenient, easy way.

Go to the Chrome web store and type in Add to any.

Add it to chrome. When you get it added it puts an icon on chrome that is the blue square with the plus sign. There are a few other programs that do this, but this is the best.

Click on the icon and go down to options and set up the sites you want to have available to add web pages or articles to. When you finish that, you are ready to go.

When you read an article, you want to add to one of those sites, click on the icon and select the site you want to add it to. Follow the prompts and in a couple of seconds you have the article added to that site. It is just that easy.

I use this to add articles to Tumblr, Blogger, Facebook, Twitter, StumbleUpon, Google plus, Delicious, Digg, and Reddit. It works well and is easy to use. Much easier than doing the copy URL, go to the site you want to add it to paste the URL and then publish it. You can add it to 5 pages at the same time as adding it to one page with the copy and paste method.

ONE TAB

One Tab is a cool extension for Google Chrome. It gives you a way to organize all the websites you use all the time into an easy-to-use bookmark type of list that is easy to access and use. It also uses less memory in the browser, but lets you access the sites you want quick and easy.

Go to the Chrome web store in Chrome. In the search box type in one tab.

Add it to Chrome. When you add it, you will see an icon in the extension box that looks like a weather balloon. That is your One-tab access.

What you can do with this program is set up groups of websites or pages you use often. You can put them into groups, so they are organized and easy to access. The cool thing about the groups is that you can open one tab you need, or you can open the whole group at one time.

For example: I have a group set up for tracking my book sales. Every night I want to see how the sales went for the day. I have in the group the pages I need to go to for tracking the book sales, a spreadsheet I use to put the numbers into, the page that tracks the ad campaigns I am running, and a currency converter page so I can see what the amount is in any currency.

When I want to see the numbers, I go to my one-tab tab, that I have pinned to a tab on my Chrome browser. I look at the tab and go down to the group for book sales. I click on restore all and it opens all the sites in that group in a couple of seconds, and I am ready to track my books.

I have several groups. I have the one for the book sales; I have one for disc golf sites, one for photography sites, one for writing sites, one for Christian sites, one for computer issues, etc. Have a group for the things you look at and are interested in. I can open one site or open them all at one time. I can set up the groups for the different computers I use as well.

You only must set it up once and it is ready to go. After you get One tab set up on your browser. Open a browser page on Chrome. Open each page you want in a group. If you want a group for entertainment. Pick Netflix, Hulu, Amazon video, MTV, etc. whatever you want in that group.

When you get them all open, click on the One-tab icon at the top right of your browser. It will move all the pages you have open into a group in the one-tab tab. Move your mouse into the group and move them around to whatever order you want. If you want them to open in a certain order when you restore all, set it up how you want.

After you get them arranged, go over to where it says more. Name the group whatever you want to make it easy to find. Click on more again and lock the group. Do not forget to lock it. If you do not lock it, the next time you hit the icon, you will add the pages to that group. If the group is locked, it creates a new group.

Go back to the main page and close the tabs open for that group. Open the tabs you want for the next group and do the same thing all over again. If you want to add to a group later, open that page, unlock the group you want it in and hit the icon, it will put it in that group. Then lock it again.

If you want to move pages in the group or delete a page, unlock it, and do what you want, and lock it again when you are done. It saves you a ton of time and memory space because you can open and close groups of websites quick and easy and only have open the ones you are using.

I have a main group also of sites I want to open most of the time I turn on the computer. I have 4 pages in that group. I have outlook, Google docs, Amazon, Wunderlist. These are pages I always have open. When I start the Chrome browser it remembers for me now, it opens a pinned tab for one tab, wunderlist, amazon, Google docs and outlook. I am ready to go. The other groups in one tab I open and close them as I need them.

Check out this program, you will love it if you use different web pages for different things at different times.

WHAT COMPUTER SHOULD I USE?

If you are reading this book, you are likely not a big computer user who uses the software you need a Mac or Windows pc. Photoshop, Illustrator and other useful, but intense software, you do not need one of those systems.

If you want a computer to surf online, look up information online, accessing Facebook, Twitter, Snapchat and other social media sites, a Chromebook is for you. If you want to watch YouTube or watch movies and TV on a computer, a Chromebook is for you. If you want a computer to organize your life and maybe a business, a Chromebook is for you.

If you want to write books or articles, and you want a computer you can carry with you, boot up fast and shut down fast, a Chromebook is for you. If you are a student, and you need to do many of the things above, but still be able to take notes on a portable computer in class and keep it organized and have a device you do not have to plug in for up to ten hours, a Chromebook is for you.

As you can tell, if you want a computer to do what most people want a computer for, a Chromebook is the best choice. I am writing this book now sitting in a chair at a cabin overlooking a beautiful lake while my wife is fishing on the dock just down the hill. We are in the middle of Minnesota away from the city having a relaxing weekend. I use my cell phone as a hotspot, so I can do anything I want to do on the internet. One of the great things with a Chromebook is I do not have to have an internet connection to do what I am doing.

Google docs works offline on the Chromebook. This allows you to do so many things without a connection. When I need a connection, I flip on my hotspot and do what I need to do. This includes saving what I am doing on the cloud. This computer is quick, has a great HD screen, and the battery lasts for ten hours.

I have a high-capacity portable drive I can download movies to at home and bring them with me to watch on the computer when I want. I can also watch things I recorded, on my dir. at home and thousands of TV shows live and thousands of shows on demand through my Chromebook streaming with the hotspot.

I also have several flash drives that are the size of a thumbnail that are 64gb in size, I can save things I want to save from the Chromebook. I have a wireless mouse hooked up. This computer is as good as any if you need not use any large software program that needs to be running on the computer. Programs like Photoshop, Illustrator, Microsoft Office, etc. If you do any video of audio editing, you use dedicated software.

I am not saying these programs are bad. I use photoshop and I use office sometimes. I use my desktop a lot. Because I do photo work, and I like the 32-inch monitor much better for those things. I will always have a desktop because of those things.

I do not sell Chromebooks. I do not care what brand you get although mine are both Acers. I like Acer because they have been making computers for a long time. They also have good prices for a good product. Explore the different brands and the features they have. Decide what you want the computer to do and go from there.

Some things I would look for.
- 4 mb ram
- No fan if you want longer battery life.

- At least 2 USB ports
- A HDMI port so you can hook to a tv.
- A HD screen. The lower res screens are not bad, but if you want to watch tv or movies on the device, go for the hd screen.
- Mine has an aluminum case. I like it better than plastic, but plastic is not bad.
- Read reviews from people who own the computer.
- If you want to use it as a tablet. You can get a flip type that the screen hinges open all the way so you can use it like a tablet.
- Price of a computer. You can get a Chromebook starting around $160. The one I am using was $271. This is ½ the cost of a windows-based computer that would be comparable.

The Chromebook is super easy to set up. It only takes a few minutes. If you use chrome as your browser on other systems, it will bring your bookmarks and apps over to the Chromebook for you. It will bring your other browser settings over. If you need to, you can clean the Chromebook out and get it back to like it was new by doing a total clean out in just a couple of minutes.

I am also not saying you cannot do photo editing and video-editing online.

There are some good online photo editors and video editors. Some of my favorite photo editors are apps on my phone.

Read through the rest of the book to see what online things you can use to take full advantage of what you can do. You can do the things in this book on a windows-based or Apple based system. Because these things are online, you do not have to worry about the operating system. The Chromebook is the way to go for most users.

CREATE A WEBSITE

Having your own website is fun for a lot of different things. You can use it for many things. There are hundreds of sites you can use create a website, many of them are free. If you are using it for a business or for making money, do not use a free site. It does not look professional and not a good look. You need to at least have your own domain.

If you want to create a fun site for personal or family use, the best and easiest site is Google sites. It is part of the Google group of programs. You can access it from Google docs.

It is by far the easiest site to create a website.

Here is how to set up your own website.

The first thing to do is to lay out what you want the site to look like.
You can do this on a piece of paper. You have a home page. That is the main page that your site will open to.

Decide what pages you want on your website.

- An About me page. Tells about you and why you made the site.
- A contact pages. This can be part of the about me page. Any contact info you want to share. Email is the best way.
- Then add other pages. As an example, if you want to set up a site for your photos. You can have a page for friends, travel, animals, family, etc. whatever you want to show on separate pages. If you want to make a site to share family news and communicate with others in the family. You can set up a page for each family, or each person in the family. You can have a page about what they are doing, pictures to show what they are doing, etc. The only limit to what you can create is your imagination and who you want to share it with.
- Decide who you want to share the page with. Do you want it for family only? Do you want the page to be public so anyone can see it?

SETTING UP YOUR SITE
- Open Google Drive
- Click on new.
- Go down to more.
- Click on Google sites. This will open a blank site to build on.

- On the top row, there is a picture of a person with a + next to it. If you want to allow others to edit the page, you can give them access here. This is nice if you want to do a family site and allow a member from each family to update their family news. Others in the family can all update their pages, and everyone will keep up on all the family news.
- Next pick a theme. Check out the different ones to see what you like best.
- You have a few font choices and colors you can use.
- Put the cursor over the page title and give your site a title. My family, or whatever you want.
- Move your mouse over the header and pick the header type.
- Go to the pages tab and click on that.
- Click on the + button so you can add pages.
- When you get to this point, you can publish. The first time you publish you have a couple other things to do. Type in what you want to call the site. Until you find a name available. You can also click in the box to not have search engines index the site. This means that only people you give the site address will access the site. If you want it public, do not click in the box.

- Click on publish. At the bottom of the screen, you can view what it looks like on the internet. Close that view and go back to the editor when you have looked it over. It is not that impressive yet, but you have a good start.
- Click on each page at the top to go to that page. Set the header type for each page. You can change the header to a picture or a design. Click on the change image in the header. You can pick from some that they have for you. You can upload a picture from your computer, or you can access photos in your Google photos albums. You can experiment with these until you get the look you want.
- Next you can go to the Home page and set up what you want the homepage to say and to show. This is the main page people will see when they come to the site. Decide what you want to be here.
- Click on the insert tab on the upper right of the screen to add content.
- You can add pictures, YouTube videos, you can add text boxes to type in anything you want. You can add a link to pictures and text. You can make lists with links. You can add files and charts, just about anything.

- Every item you add will have a box pop up on the top where you can create a link or change other attributes. On the far left there is another box that will let you change the background of the object.
- You can do just about anything and create a site to share anything you want to, and it works well.

Just hit the publish button anytime you change something, and it goes live on the internet. After you publish the site, go to the home page, and copy that web address. That is the address you want to give to the people you want to share the site with.

The website will be saved in your Google Drive, so accessing it to change the site is easy and fun. This is not for a business or a site you want to make money from the internet, but if you are reading this book, that is not likely your goal. This is for personal use you want to do for free and you need no experience to set up. It makes a functional and nice website.

Here is a book website I created with this method to get people to my books. It only took me a short time, and it is functional and effective. It also looks good on a mobile device.

As far as I know, there is no limit on the number of websites you can create. So have fun and create websites for whatever you want to share.

WORDPRESS

If you are blogging for a business, or you want your own domain, WordPress is the way to go. Wordpress.org is the leading web software for blogging and for website building for businesses. WordPress is powerful and will allow you to do just about anything you want online. You can even run a store with WordPress.

I am only mentioning this, so you know the difference. Wordpress.com is a different deal. You can use Wordpress.com for your personal blog and website.

Go to WordPress pick the .com side for a personal site.

- Pick what type of page you want. A blog, a website, a store, or a portfolio if you want to show off your photography or artwork.
- Pick a theme. You can change it later, just pick one.
- Pick a name. The site will give you a URL. It will show you the free one at the top. It will recommend others that will cost you money.

- Pick a plan. If you are just starting and want a personal website, pick the free option. You can change this later.
- Put in your email and select a password.
- It will give you the URL for your site and let you go see it.
- To see how to edit your site. Check this site out.

This is a good way to get started with a blog or a website. You can experiment and use this site for anything you want on the internet.

Read the terms of service so you know what you can and cannot do. There are restrictions on the .com site.

GOOGLE PHOTOS

Google photo is one of the most awesome things there is on the internet. You can store all your photos. You can search for photos by a person, place, objects, etc.

I have taken over 600,000 photos over the past years and I have them all stored on Google Photo. I can find them so much easier in there. You can set up the program to upload your photos to Google photo. You can also store the photos in albums for easy finding later.

You can set up as many albums as you need. I have them for different trips. I have them for different locations I have been to. I have fish pictures, people pictures, animal pictures, etc. The coolest thing is the search capabilities.

Go to photos.google.com. Set up a photo account by logging in with your Google account. At the top there are two choices, create and upload. Select create and create an album, or one of the other choices. Create albums for the pictures you want to store.

The other option is upload. Click upload and you can pick a file or a folder you want to upload the photos from. It will upload your photos and then ask you if you want them in an album. Select the album and they will be there.

You can also move them from album to album.

If you want to see a picture of someone and you know when the shot was taken. You can look at the timeline on the right side and slide the slide down to when you think the shot was taken. Another way is to go to albums. On the top of the page there should be a group called people if you created one. Click on that album and it will open it up to where you can see all the people.

Click on the photo of the person you want to see. It will search through all the pictures you have, and it will pull up all the shots of that person you have. It is not perfect, but it is amazing how well it works.

You can also access all your pictures from any device you want. A great example. I was with my wife in Orlando a couple weeks ago. We were at Epcot and we walked past a statue fountain of Zeus. I took a picture of my wife in front of the fountain. I then went into Google photos and found a shot I took at the same spot of her and my stepdaughter in the same place in 1991. I sent a copy of the new photo and the one from 1991 to her and said, remember this. It only took me a minute to find. Instead of looking through all the digital shots and film shots. The original shot was on film and I scanned it.

You can store the photos full size or at a reduced size to save space. You can buy space cheap. Store them at full size and you will always have a good copy. I store my shots on Google photos and on 2 external hard drives. I also have about half of them stored on DVD's.

Some other cool things you can do with Google Photo.
- Create animations. You can make quick animations of photos by combining several photos together and the system will run through them as an animation. You can also use it to make a quick slideshow of related shot.
- A useful thing you can do is create a collage of photos you want together. You can use 2 to 9 pictures to make a collage. The only bad thing about this is that you cannot choose where it puts the shots.

- Create albums to store your related photos in. You can create albums for any types of shot you want to find.
- Create a slideshow. You need to have the photos in an album. Open the album and click on a photo in the album. Click the three dots in the upper right of the screen and select slideshow.

You can use the website on your computers and get an app on your phones and tablets.

AMAZON PHOTO

Go to Amazon and go to accounts and lists. Go down to prime photos. You can store your photos on Amazon.

Click on the add button at the top and upload. Simple to use and works well. If you have a Prime account.

Amazon photo and Google photo are both great. Most of the time I use them both. It saves all the shots I take with my phone. That way I always have 3 copies saved in different places.

I also save them on an external hard drive on my computer. But having Google and Amazon store them before I can save them on my hard drive means I will not lose any photos, no matter what happens.

You can also access your photos anywhere. You can access them from an app on your phone or tablet. You can also access them from Amazon website on any device you can access the internet.

COMPUTER TERMS

Some of these terms you hear, and you do not want to look like you know nothing about computers, so you act like you know what they mean. There is nothing wrong with not knowing everything. The terms change and new ones are added all the time. You do not have to know what all the terms mean, but it is nice to know.

VPN— It stands for Virtual private network. It gives you more security because it adds a layer of security from anyone seeing what you are doing, or where you are going on the internet. The VPN creates an encrypted tunnel between your network and the sites you are going to. No one can get into the tunnel from anywhere outside. Even your ISP cannot see where you are going.

The ip address looks like it is coming from the VPN server instead of your computer.

There are still ways you can be tracked where you have been online. Many sites use cookies to see what you are doing and what you are looking at. Some of this is not a problem and will never cause a problem. It is the big players on the internet finding out what you are doing and selling that info to advertisers to target their ads to people looking for their products.

This is creepy sometimes when you search for something on Amazon. Then you go to Google and search for that or something else, and the ads you see on the side of the pages are what you were just looking at on Amazon.

Protecting your data and your information is the biggest issue. Security is a big thing on the internet. A VPN could be the best thing for you. There are several services available. The cost is around $10 per month for the top ones. Here is a link to pc mags top vpn's

Wi Fi. One of the big things I see people do not understand is how Wi-Fi and how internet works. Internet is what you get from your service provider to your house. The speed you get will not be what you get for a Wi-Fi signal. If you get 100 mbps coming to your modem, you get that to your devices if you are plugging them in with an ethernet cable direct.

If you are using Wi-Fi, which everyone does for many things. That is where things can change a lot.

The router sends out a Wi-Fi signal, and it goes into the air. The signal is put out in a spherical pattern. Many things will affect what speed you get at your Wi-Fi devices. Putting your router in the center of your living space is the ideal place for it. Many times, that is not possible.

As the signal goes out, many things can affect the quality and speed. One of the biggest is interference from other networks. If you look at your mobile phone and see what networks your phone sees, you can see several. If you live in an apartment complex, you could see 30 networks or more. All those signals your phone sees are causing interference on your network. 2.4 gb will have more interference than a 5 gb network. There are fewer users and there are more 5gb channels than 2.4 channels that you can use.

Other things that will affect your Wi-Fi are cordless phones and microwaves. They both operate on the same frequency. Another big thing that affects the signal is distance. The 2.4 gb network has a longer range but is not as fast and has more interference than the 5 gb network.

If you are having issues with Wi-Fi, there are things you can do. The best options are to make sure you have an updated modem. The second is setting up a mesh system in your house. A mesh system is like a range extender but much better. The pieces of a mesh system work together to get you the best Wi-Fi all over your house. Range extenders pick up your Wi-Fi signal and amplify it and try to send it out farther. A mesh system talks to all pieces in the system. There are 3 or more parts to a mesh system. Each one can talk to the router and to each of the other parts to get you the best signal throughout your house.

There are other things you can do if you are having Wi-Fi issues. I have written a book on Wi-Fi and what I did to make my system work like a charm You can check it out here.

SOCIAL MEDIA

Social media is a term we use and hear used for a lot of things. The meaning of social media is a vague and somewhat generic term, it is kind of like Kleenex. Kleenex is a brand name but almost everyone calls any facial tissue a Kleenex.

Social media was a term that was used when Myspace and Twitter and Facebook were starting. It has evolved to cover all kinds of blog sites and other sharing sites. It is a broad term. Social is interacting and communicating with others, and media is the way to communicate and share with others.

Social media is pretty much anything on the internet that people use to communicate with other and share their beliefs and ideas. This section will cover the main so-called social media sites. Several other sections of the book could also be classified as social media sites.

I will cover the basics of how to use.
- Facebook
- Twitter
- Google Plus
- Instagram

- Pinterest
- Reddit
- Tweet Deck, a better way to use Twitter.
- StumbleUpon

I know there are many more that many people consider social media. I am not covering any of the sites that are chat sites and call sites. This is for multimedia type sharing and finding information. Enjoy.

FACEBOOK

Facebook is the most popular social media site. It is easy to set up and easy to keep track of your family and friends. It is also a great way to keep up with company information and new products and news. I follow several companies so I can see what is going on with them and what they have coming out.

To set up your Facebook page
- Open the Facebook homepage and enter your information.
- Click sign up at the bottom.
- You will get a confirmation email. Click the link to confirm you gave a valid email address.
- Then set up your profile.
- Enter a profile picture.
- Add friends.
- Set privacy setting to show who can see your posts.
- You are ready to post.

You can post messages, photos, links to websites, etc.
You can share events you are having or attending.

Facebook is a good way to stay in touch with family and friends if they are not close to you.

There are things I dislike about Facebook. The ads they have are annoying and sometimes you cannot even see the stories you are trying to read. Many times, I end up saying heck with it and go on to something else. I have thought about just not using Facebook because of the ads. I get too much information from Facebook to not use it.

Once you have an account, you can set up pages. The pages are for dealing with specific things you believe, or you are promoting. A business or hobby you want to connect with like-minded people. I have several I used to share information about the things I am passionate about. Bass fishing, kayak fishing, fishing in MN, Christian issues, Internet stuff, Disc golf, Photography and exercise and fitness.

Pages are easy to create also.
Below the listings on the left side of the page there is a link that says create.
- Click on create a page.
- Select what type of page you want to create. You have six options. Pick the one that fits your page.

- Read the Facebook tips and do the things it tells you to do for your page.
- Share with your friends and people you want to see the page.

Some people get lots of followers and lots of people they follow. Pages are a great way to share with specific people. A good example is a family page. Set up a page for your family. Invite all the members of your family and extended family you want to follow, and you can follow them. Family members can post information on the page to alert other family members of things they are doing or want others to do with them. You can go to the page and see only things with your family any time you want.

Your pages will be listed on the left side of your regular Facebook page. Just click on the page you want to see, and you can add or read other posts anytime.

TWEETDECK

Tweet deck is a cool program you can run on your computer. The cool thing about it is that you can have it show each of your lists in a separate column. It makes it much easier to see the tweets you want to see when you want to see them.

There is so much information being tweeted around the clock, there is no way to keep up with what you want to see. Tweet deck lets you organize the tweets in columns and sort it by your twitter lists. I love this program for accessing the info you want on twitter.

There are several other things you can do through the program.
- You can tweet on twitter.
- You can search twitter and create a new column and or list.
- You can access different accounts.
- You can move people to and from lists.

Most of the things I do on Twitter, I do from Tweet deck.

The key to making tweet deck work is to have all the people and twitter accounts you want to follow in lists. The lists show up in columns in tweet deck, so they are easy to follow.

I follow close to 4,000 on Twitter, and close to that many following me. It is beyond what you can reasonably manage without tweet deck. I have 20 lists and most of the ones I follow are in a list. Tweet deck has twenty columns that show me the tweets separated, I can look at just the topics I want to see.

Also set up a main feed and an activity feed. So, you can see all the feeds coming in and you can see all the posts you make in their own column.

Go to tweet deck and set up your account. You then connect it to twitter from there.

GOOGLE PLUS

Google plus has recently shut down. Not sure if it is coming back but here is how to use it.
Google plus is kind of like Facebook, but it is more of a sharing thing. More of a community site to share what people like. I follow many photographers on Google plus; they post photos they take. There are tons of great photographers all over the world and it is fun to see the shots they take.

Google hangouts is integrated into Google plus, and Gmail. It lets you make phone calls, video calls and chats with up to 100 people at a time. The hangouts are where you can be part of a community for any topic. You can use an app on your phone or connect through a computer with hangouts.

If you have a Google account, you are ready to go. **Go to Google plus** and log in with your Google account to get started. When you access the site on a computer, it looks like Pinterest. When you access it on your phone, it looks more like Facebook.

Go to the home button and set up your profile and get ready to get acquainted. If you get lost on the site, just hit the home button to get back to this page where your news feed is.

- HOME This is where you find your news feed of the people you are following. Like Facebook only it looks like Pinterest.
- DISCOVER This is where you go to find new people to follow and new topics you are interested in.
- COMMUNITIES This where you go to see the communities you are part of. Example: Portrait photography, Bass fishing, etc.
- PROFILE This is where you can edit your profile and see the posts you have posted to your news feed.
- CIRCLES This is where you see the people in your circles. Where you and your friends go. Kind of like groups in Facebook, but easier to organize and keep track of. If you click on the find people button, it will open suggestions for you. When you find someone you want to add, hover over their name and it will give you choices of which circle to add them to. You can connect to people you do not know yet. If you click on the button at the top of that page that says added you, you can see people who have added you to their circles, and you can add them back.

- **POSTING** There are a few different ways you can post to Google plus. When you are on your homepage, or any other page with posts, you will see a rep pen in the lower right corner. Click on that and you can create a post. You can also post articles you see from many websites or an extension to Chrome called add to any.

When you get on the site, go to communities, or discover. Pick the communities you want to follow and follow good posts. You can join in and post things you have that other will enjoy. It is easy to post, just tap in the spot that says what is new with you?

Getting around on the site is easy to do. I do most of my checking out the site on my phone that way I can save the best stuff for looking at later. Great photos are also nice to keep in a swipe file so you can try to create a similar shot later.

Because of how Google plus works, there are things you want to make sure you do or do not do.

- Because it is a social network, make sure you complete your profile, so everyone knows who you are.
- Do not load up your profile with keywords to get more people to check out your stuff. Make sure the keywords are related to your topics.
- Make sure you use a good cover image on Your Google plus page.
- Use your circles as they call groups.
- Do not spam your circles.
- Answer negative comments.
- Join a community.
- Put up a picture on your profile.

Circles are a way to organize the people you connect with, or your groups. You can have a circle for family, one for friends, one for things you do for hobbies, etc. A group of people you want to share certain information with and not with everyone.

To start a circle, go to your Google plus, click on the people link. Then click on following and go to the bottom and click on the new circle. Create a circle you want and add other people to your circle.

To add or remove someone from a circle, go to the profile of that person and click on circles. Add or move them to another circle.

Once you get circles set up for things and people you want to follow, go to discover, and find people and subjects to follow and put them in your circles. This is like Tweet Deck lets you do with people on twitter.

There are mobile apps you can download to your phone to do everything on mobile devices.

TWITTER

Twitter is a popular form of social media. It is a good way to communicate short blurbs of information be it personal or business. You can get a lot of followers and follow many people. Once you get to where you are following hundreds or thousands of people, it can get way out of control and overwhelming. This happened when I got to around 1000 people I followed and followed me.

This is where Tweet Deck will save you. Look at the Tweet Deck chapter and set it up at the beginning, it will make your life much easier.

USING TWITTER
- Go to the Twitter homepage and set up a twitter account.
- Follow the prompts. It is easy to do.
- You pick a username.
- You pick a password.
- Finish the sign up and click create my account.
- Pick some subjects you are interested in.
- Pick some people and companies to follow.
- Put them into lists right away. When you are following them, click on the 3 dots next to

their follow button and put them into a list. This will make it easy to find the information later.

To set up lists, go to the top of homepage and click on your name or picture, then click on lists in the center of the screen. Here you can see your lists and see how many you are following in each list. You can click on the list and see the tweets from the ones you follow in that list only. This is where Tweet Deck makes it great. You can see all your lists separated on one page.

Keep looking for people and things you are interested in and follow them. If people follow you, check out what they tweet and follow them back if it interests you. Do not follow back if it is not something you want to see. If you do, you will get a lot of tweets you do not care about.

INSTAGRAM

Instagram is one of the most popular social media sites. It is easy to use and useful for staying in contact with friends and people you want to follow. Instagram is owned by Facebook. The biggest difference is it is photos and videos and not so much the blog type format like Facebook.

- Download the app to your phone or tablet, tap on the Instagram icon to open it.
- Tap on what form you want to use to register. Email, Facebook.
- Click on the person on the bottom right to edit your profile.
- Enter your information to create your account.

Navigating Instagram
- You can add pictures to Instagram from the camera on the top left side, or you can add photos from your camera roll.
- To add from your camera roll, click on the icon in the bottom toolbar with the + inside it.
- You can also add photos from the picture of you in the top bar.

- Use the magnifying glass to search for people to follow.
- Use the magnifying glass to look at the photos and videos below to see others to follow.
- The home tab shows your news feed where all the posts show up.
- You can click on the icons across the top and see what each of the people you follow have posted.
- If you want to stop following someone. Click on their post and click in the 3 dots on the top right of their post and pick unfollow.
- You can send direct messages to others if you tap on the icon at the top right that looks like a paper airplane.
- Once you get your account set up, you can also access it from the web without using the app. The online version is the same. The Instagram symbol in the upper left is your home button. The circle with the symbol inside it is the explore icon. If you go to the home screen and click on your picture, you can see your posts and who you follow and who follows you.

Instagram is a useful quick way to post from your phone and stay in contact with friends and family.

PINTEREST

Pinterest is one of my favorite sites for getting information. It is pictures and information for pretty much anything you are looking for. The best thing about Pinterest is that it is visual. Lots of pictures and illustrations covering the subject you are researching.

Go to Pinterest and set up an account. Once you get started, search for something you are interested in. When you find tutorials or articles or illustrations of what you want to save for later use, click on the save button at the upper right.

This will take you to a page that asks you to pick the board you want to save it to. You create boards you want to have things saved to.

As an example. I typed in bass fishing jigs. It pulls up hundreds of picture articles about bass fishing with jigs. Types of jigs, how to rig the jigs, etc. I can then click on interesting articles or pictures and open them up. I read them and if I want to save it for future reference; I click on the save button and save it to my bass fishing jig board.

If you use Pinterest a lot, you can set up your own internet with the things you are interested in and be able to go to it anytime you want.

Another example. I am learning to draw. One of the hardest things to draw is human hands. I type in how to draw hands and I get hundreds of tutorials with pictures and step-by-step instructions to draw hands.

Pinterest is also a great way to share information you know and want to share with others. Create your boards and post things you create and things you find on other sites. Everyone shares great info on the subjects they are interested in and everyone benefits. You can also comment and re pin others pins to get more exposure to the boards of interest and share knowledge you have.

Check it out, you will be glad you did.

REDDIT

Reddit is huge and growing fast. There are close to 250 million users worldwide. They call themselves the front page of the internet. It is a great place to find up-to-date content on just about anything you can imagine. Facebook and Twitter have been that for a long time. Reddit has taken off over the past 5 years and is up there with the others.

At first look Reddit seems to be a mess of hard to navigate posts. If you want access to a world of information, it is worth learning to use it. Reddit is the main site. A subreddit is a section of the page that deals with specific topics. There is a subreddit for anything you can think of. It is not for everyone. Check it out and see if you think it is worth it.

Go to reddit.com You can look around on the front page and see if there is anything you are interested in. The way to get to the stuff you want to see is to search for a subreddit that has the topic you are looking for.

The site is a giant forum. Most forums are for a particular topic. Reddit is thousands of forums combined into one. People who view on Reddit vote up or down if they like or dislike posts. This makes Reddit a changing and evolving group of topical information. When you first get there, you will feel like there is no organization and no-good information.

At the top of the page is a toolbar that says my subreddits. The arrow on there is a drop-down box that will show you the subreddits, scroll down and pick one that looks interesting. It also lists them in the toolbar going across the screen. If you cannot find something interesting, or you do not have saved subreddits, click on the popular, or news or any of the other ones on the list and see what you get. There is even a random button that just picks something random and takes you there.

You can also click on the end of the drop-down or the end of the toolbar where it says edit. You will get a box that asks, what are you interested in? Type into the box and it will give you what it is you are looking for, or a subreddit that should have the topic you are looking for.

When you find ones you want to go back to, subscribe to them and they will be in your subreddits for return visits. In each thread there are topics you can read and interact with the other people in the thread on things you want to ask or discuss.

Example. If I want to find information on bass fishing in Minnesota. I type in bass fishing Minnesota. It gives links to try for fishing Minnesota. I click on that and it pulls up a page with questions about what to use, where to fish, what to bring on trips, about fishing in Minnesota. You can also ask for advice on what you want to do. If you are going fishing in the BWCA and you want to know how to fish, there. You can ask and you will get lots of good advice on what to use and where to fish.

If you want to get advice and read people's ideas and comments about topics, reddit is a good place to hang out. It is also good if you like to give advice and help people find out the information they are looking for.

If you want to subscribe and take part, you need to sign up and create an account. It is easy to do.

You can also follow people on reddit if you find interesting people you want to learn from, or just see what they have to say. There is so much here that you can get lost for hours checking out different topics. You can also get into some great interaction with other like-minded people.

One thing I do not like about Reddit is you can only do things so often. It limits you on adding content or even commenting on things. You can only do things so often if it thinks you are doing too much it says you have to wait. That makes little sense. I like to go on the photography site and answer questions on photos. Photographers take shots and ask for advice on what they can do to make their shots better. You should be able to comment more than every 10 or 15 minutes.

The best way to use reddit is through the app. The app works well for mobile use. The navigation is easier, and you can get to what you want faster. I use it on the app unless I am commenting on photos. Do not like to type a lot on the phone. If you want to explore and see a lot of cool photos and videos, use the app.

You can use Reddit by doing a few different things. Go to your subreddits page and clean up the junk. Things you would not be interested in.

STUMBLEUPON

StumbleUpon has been one of my favorite sites when I want to look at articles or pictures on a specific subject. You can pick to stumble through random subjects, or you can just see posts on one idea.

Go to stumble upon and sign up for an account. Set up the subjects you are interested in exploring. When you go to the site, you pick the subject you want to see, or you can just hit the stumble button and it will pick any of the subjects you have selected.

You can also post information you want to share with others on the site as well. It is kind of like a whole internet of just what you are looking for.

BLOGGING

You can use a personal blog for many things. It can be like a Facebook page for you. It can be a way to get out information about something you want to share info with other people.

You can use it for a family notification. You can even use it for storing information you want to store for yourself.

This is how I use blogs. I use blogger blogs to store information on things I wanted to save for me to access when I wanted to. Kind of like my personal internet. I have a blog on bass fishing where I clip good articles that I read and want to save for later. I have over 10,000 posts on that blog, covering every aspect of bass fishing. I can search it and find what I am looking for.

After a while I saw that thousands of other people were visiting my blog and reading the articles I was saving. Several thousand per month. This is a great way to share info that other people are interested in. It is cool because people from all around the world are reading my posts.

There are many uses to a blog. It is only limited by your imagination and what you want to save, or what you think other people will want to see. You can add in your own posts as well and reach all those readers with information you want to share.

START YOUR OWN BLOG

Blogging is something that many people want to do, and many more would like to try. Blogging is a great way to get information to many people in an easy format.

A blog also works great for a family site. You can put information on the blog and the rest of your family can go there and find out what everyone is doing. You can let everyone in the family have access so everyone can add to the blog.

You can have a blog about a hobby. You can blog about your work. You can blog about anything you believe in or want to share your opinions with other people. You can use a blog to store articles for yourself to read or to use. You can have a blog That is public or private. There are hundreds of things you can use a blog for.

There are a lot of places you can set up a blog. The most used blogging software is a program called WordPress. The software is great and is used by millions of people. To use it you need to have your own website. Most people who want to create a blog for their personal use and family and sharing things with friends do not need to get a web hosting service. The version you download to your site is at Wordpress.org.

There is a version of WordPress that is free.
Wordpress.com
You can set up a blog or a website at WordPress. The free version gives you a website or blog site on their server. You can pick a name, but it is not a domain name. It is a subdomain on their site. It will be a name like Bobjones.wordpress.com.

You can upgrade and get a domain name of your own. There is a cost for that and then you must have it hosted on a site. There is a charge for that. For a blog for family or just information sharing about a hobby or interest the free site will work.

If you are starting and want to try it out. Use the free version and see what it is all about. It is easy to sign up and easy to create a website or a blog. It takes a little work, but it is easy with trial and error. Blogging is easy, you can be up and blogging in half an hour or less.

Another great blog site for free is **Blogger.com**. I prefer blogger, you can do more with it and it is easy to set up and work. **Here is a blog I have set up on Blogger** I use it to share photography articles I find that have great information about photography with other photographers. Google runs this site. People find these sites and visit them. If you want to set up a public site and get viewers, Blogger is the way to go.

I have 17 blogs setup like this one on Blogger. I get tens of thousands of viewers on the blogs. I have the side adds for my books on there as well, but it is great information I am sharing with other like-minded people. You can also sign up for an AdSense account and make money from people clicking on ads on your page. That is for another book.

When you get set up for a blog on Blogger. It tracks stats as to visitors for you. It shows you where they are, so you can see what parts of the world you are reaching. You can go to the admin page and set up a theme for how you want the blog to look. You can set colors, and size of the columns. There are widgets you can use to add things like lists and links. You can set up pages so you can have a special page for different things you want to share other info for, or about you, etc. You can add pictures, etc. Just about anything you want to do, you can do with this software.

Because these sites are free and are run by others, you have rules you need to follow. Make sure you read the rules for content in the help section, so you do not violate the rules of the sites. If you violate the rules, they will just cancel your account, be careful. Another cool thing you can do on Blogger is if you use Chrome as your browser, you can download an extension that will put the articles you select from the internet links on the blog you want. Easy.

There are many other sites out there that you can use for blogging that I am sure work well. These are the biggest and I feel Blogger is the best for most people for general blogging. If you will be using it for a business or something where you want to make money from the blog, do not use the free sites, get your own domain, and use WordPress on your own site.

SETTING UP YOUR BLOG ON BLOGGER
- Create an account and start a new blog.
- Type in a title for your blog
- Type in an address for your blog until you find one not used.

- Pick a theme. You can change it anytime so do not be too picky here. Just pick something.
- Click on create blog.
- You will come to the main edit page. This is where you do most of your work.
- Click on view the blog and you will see what it looks like
- Close that and go back to edit page.
- Go down to theme and click on that.
- Click customize below your theme.
- This is where you pick your theme. There are a lot of choices here. This can take a while to go through each. I recommend you lay out a design on a mind map program, or a piece of paper. Look at other blogs. Decide if you want one, two, or three columns and what you want in each column. You can change this anytime, but once you add content it will look much different in different themes. if you change the number of columns. Come up with a design of what you want now.
- Remember to keep it as simple so it looks good. If you have too much going on, or if you have a background that looks cool, it may make the blog hard to read. You want to make it easy on the eyes and easy to read.

- Go back to edit page and click on layout. Scroll down and click on add a gadget under the column you want to add the gadget. Follow the directions in the gadget and see what they do. I like to use the image one. You can put in a picture and have it link to somewhere else. Like to a website or a web page or anywhere you want.
- Hit save arrangement and view blog to see what it looks like.
- You can remove any gadgets you do not want by clicking in the gadget on the edit link and delete it.
- The next thing you should do is get posts on the blog. You can type them in or if you install the blogger extension on chrome, you can send them to your blog from most websites. When you find a recipe you want to save, right click on the picture of the food. Then select a piece of text from the recipe or do not select text. If you select text, do not copy it, just leave it selected. This puts a little text in the blog post. It looks better.
- Then click on the blogger icon on the chrome browser. A window will pop up for blogger, in the upper right corner there is a drop-down box if you have more than one blog. Select the blog you want to post to. Click in

the post box and hit enter. Right click in the space above the link and paste the picture. At the bottom of the picture, you can size the picture. Large or medium is the best. At the bottom you can hit publish and it is on your blog with a picture, the text you highlighted and a link to the webpage.

- If you have your own recipes you want to put on the site, you can go to the edit page and click on new post and do it all from there.
- You can share this page with whoever you want, and they can access it when you want a recipe.
- You can experiment with other things and with gadgets and you can set up this blog to be useful for many things, only limited by you.
- You can grab the gadgets and move them around to anywhere you want. You can even move them to different sidebars.
- If you make a mistake, you can go to the edit page and click on posts and edit any post you want.
- If you have multiple blogs, do not forget to change the blog you want to post to in the upper right corner before you publish. You do not want to post something on a blog that is unrelated.

As with websites, if you are doing this for a business, or you want to be making money from your blog, this is not the way to go. But if you want a blog to share info and even just put your opinions out there. Blogger is the way to go. The website clipper is a useful tool for sharing and saving things you want to access.

TUMBLR

Tumblr is the fastest growing social media site. It is
caused some problems for the site. They were
having a hard time keeping up with the increasing
volume. Tumblr is a micro blog site that is between
a blog and twitter. You can use more characters
than Twitter, but it is for short blogs or ideas.

You can use Tumblr to blog or you can use it to
follow others and get information about anything
you want. It is like Facebook in that you can post
things longer than twitter, but it is more enjoyable
because you do not have ads popping up all the
time. You can also click on things and read them
without having to go through so many ads you give
up. Many things on Facebook I want to read are not
worth going through 25 pages of ads to read.

To post on your own blogs is quite easy as well. You
can also have the post set up in a queue so it will
post later. You can set up several posts to go out
later, so they are not altogether.

You can set up a blog for anything you want and
post short posts that you can use to communicate
your ideas and likes. You can use text, video, or

photos in your blogs. You can follow other bloggers with similar interests.

Go to tumblr.com and set up an account.

Learn the types of posts.
- Text. A text post can have text, images, links, and videos. Not just text.
- Photos. This is a photo with a short description. You can upload your photo, or you can use the URL of an online photo.
- Quote. This is the quote, and then a line to describe where the quote is from.
- Link. A description of what the link is with the link.
- Chat. Used to share a piece of conversation.
- Audio. A mp3 file. Can be music, podcast, etc. Can only post one audio post per day.
- Video. An embedded video. Can be from your computer or from YouTube or Vimeo.

Follow people and get followers.
- Go to your home page.
- On the right sidebar, look at the recommended people to follow. See if any of those interest you.
- On the bottom of that section, click on the explore all Tumblr.

- The bar across the top has different categories to look through for blogs to follow.
- That is all there is to it for following.

On the home page.
- There are icons on the upper right of the page.
- You can send messages, receive messages, create posts, etc.
- If you have more than one blog, clicking on the account icon will show you how to access your other blogs.

Once you are set up, Tumblr is easy to use and easy to follow. You can get stuck for hours looking at posts and reposting them and wasting time.

WORDPRESS

If you are blogging for a business, or you want your own domain, WordPress is the way to go. Wordpress.org is the leading web software for blogging and for website building for businesses. WordPress is powerful and will allow you to do just about anything you want online. You can even run a store with WordPress.

I am only mentioning this, so you know the difference. Wordpress.com is a different deal. You can use Wordpress.com for your personal blog and website.

Go to WordPress pick the .com side for a personal site.

- Pick what type of page you want. A blog, a website, a store, or a portfolio if you want to show off your photography or artwork.
- Pick a theme. You can change it later.
- Pick a name. The site will give you a URL. It will show you the free one at the top. It will recommend others that will cost money.

- Pick a plan. If you are just starting and want a personal website, pick the free option. You can change this later.
- Put in your email and select a password.
- They system will give you the URL for your site and let you go see it.
- To see how to edit your site. Check this site.

This is a good way to get started with a blog or a website. You can experiment and use this site for anything you want on the internet.

Read the terms of service so you know what you can and cannot do. There are restrictions on the .com site.

BACKING UP YOUR COMPUTER

Keeping your computer backed up is something that is important if you have files on it, you cannot afford to lose. If you are using a Chromebook, you do not have this issue, but if you use any windows-based computer, you need to back it up.

There are easy and harder ways for backing up your computers. The easy ways are the best because you do not have to think about them. If it is something you need to remember to do, you will forget for sure. Several services do the backup for you, so you do not have to remember to back it up yourself.

Carbonite is the one I use, because I have used it for several years, and it works without me having to do anything. If it is not broke, do not fix it.

CARBONITE

Carbonite was the first cloud backup service. They have been around since 2005. Carbonite is easy to set up and to use. The system backs up all your important files and photos, without you needing to do anything. You can also access them from any web connected device.

It takes a while when you first get it going; it must upload all the files you want to back up. The faster your internet connection the faster the backup. Once it gets started, it only backs up what changes. And it does it in the background, so you notice nothing happening.

The basic home plan is plenty for most people. The pricing is $59 per year for one computer. Carbonites cost $5 per month is worth the price. You can also backup external drives for about twice the price. **Check out their website here.** The cost goes up for multiple computers. $269 per year.

This is the service I have used for several years. I backup my main computer and my external hard drive for $99 per year. I make sure I save everything on my laptop on the cloud and on my desktop or external hard drive. My desktop is my main computer with my external drives. That is the computer I keep backed up.

CLOUD ONLINE BACKUP

Backing up your important files is something everyone should do. You can do it yourself, and it will work. The problem doing it yourself is that you will not remember to do it all the time. You can do it to the cloud on your own. Still, you may not be up to date, and it takes work to get all your files and photos updated in the cloud.

What are the backup options you have?

You can do a manual backup.
- Use cd's, DVDs, or a Blu-ray player to save your critical files.
- You can use an external hard drive.
- You can use an online cloud service.

You can use an online cloud backup service. These services do not just copy your files when you remember. They back up your files when you change them without you doing anything. You need not remember to do it. Backing up your drive is important. You do not know when you will get a virus, or your hard drive will die.

Online backups protect you from viruses and malware. It also protects from a hard drive failure or a stolen computer. Some things are replaceable, some are not. If you save photos on your devices all the time and do not get backups right away, you could lose them. I have used backup services for many years. I had to use the restore only one time, but it was easy and great to get it all back.

There are many services out there for backup services. I am sure there are others as good as the ones I have listed here. These are the top ones and the ones you can use and feel confident you will get the service you need.

BACKBLAZE

Back blaze is a service I have used. This service is a one computer setup like Carbonite. I Make sure I store all my important files on the cloud. On my hard drive, on my external hard drive and with an online automatic backup service.

Back blaze cost $5 per month for one computer. I only need one computer backed up to protect my files. The other computers I store all the important files online. I store most of my files on Evernote, on Google Docs on my external drive, and on Carbonite. The one thing Back blaze does not give you is access to your files anywhere for just access. You can download and restore files from any location, but you cannot get to them just for access. That is normally not an issue since you can access all your files from any device on several other storage sites.

IDRIVE

I Drive at first look appears to be a better deal. If you have several computers and other devices you want to back up, it is better. After you look deeper into the plans, they may not be better for what you need covered.

I Drive has a free plan that gives you up to 5gb of storage. That you will fill quick, but if you do not have a lot to back up, it could work for you.

Their lowest plan starts with a first-year discount, but it doubles the second year. Check out their plans and see what works for you.

MEGA

Mega backup is a good deal for most people. There is no limit on the amount you can back up. You can also access your files from anywhere at a fair price. They store all the files on Amazon web service, which is huge. Amazon stores an unbelievable amount of data on their servers, and they know what they are doing.

They have a special if you pay for 24mo of service, it is $95, or $3.95 per month. You can also share files with anyone. I have not tried this service and I only know what I have read about this service, but it looks good and it has a decent price. Check out their site here.

SOS ONLINE
BACKUP

It is an editor's choice for PC magazine. It gives you everything you need to keep all your data backed up and secure. You can back up five devices. The amount and the number of files is unlimited. They offer a 15-day free trial to see if it works for you. Their base price is $4.99mo for 50gb. Adding more storage raises the cost.

This is a good service and will work well if you do not have a lot to back up.

Check their site and see what you think.

CONCLUSION

There are literally millions of things to do on the internet to make things in your life better and easier. The problem is most people do not have time to learn how to use it all.

This book is a way to help you get around the big learning curve and learn to do things to help you keep organized and make your life easier.

ABOUT ME

My name is Steve Pease. I live in the Northern suburbs of the Twin Cities in Minnesota.

I have been writing for about six years. I have written several hundred articles for Hub Pages and for examiner over the years. For Examiner I wrote a column for the Twin Cities on Disc golf, and one on Cycling in the Twin Cities, and one on Exercise and fitness for the Twin cities.

I write on subjects I am passionate about, disc golf, exercise, photography, cycling, fishing, and topics that deal with Christian beliefs.

My father is a retired minister, and he has written many books. I have edited many of them and have them available on my site that cover many topics of interest to Christians today. I have also written an Old Testament trivia book on my own.

I have been playing disc golf since 1978 and love the sport. The greatest thing about disc golf is at age sixty I am still extremely competitive and beat players much younger than me. Disc golf is a sport you can play at almost any age if you can walk.

I have taken several hundred thousand pictures over the last 35 years and I am always trying to improve my photography. My goal is always to take the best shots I can. I want people to say wow when they look at my shots. I went through the photography course at New York Institute of photography many years ago. What I learned from the course and my years of experience was worth every dollar.

The key to be a great photographer is to see things that most people do not see, or in a way they did not see it. My favorite types of photography are landscape, portrait, animals and infrared. I have shot several weddings and spend hundreds of hours just exploring different places looking for great things to take pictures of.

I have been an avid fisherman since I was a kid. I have had 2 bass fishing boats over the years, but I enjoy fishing from my kayak. I have a sit inside old town kayak, and a sit on top feelfree Moken 12 fishing kayak. I also have two old town canoes for going to the boundary waters wilderness area or just paddling around lakes in my area.

 The hardest part about fishing from a kayak is trying to decide what not to take with me. As with most bass fishermen I have tons of equipment, and I always feel I need to take it all with me, just in case. Kayak fishing has made me downsize just to make everything fit in my kayak.

I spend most of my fishing time catching bass and northern pike. But if I am looking for a good meal, you can beat crappies and sunfish. I have spent most of my time fishing freshwater, but I have caught saltwater fish. The biggest was a 380-pound bull shark off Key West Florida in 1985.

I have also loved biking and exercising since I was in my early teens. I like to read nonfiction book so I can keep learning new things all the time. Many of the things I learn I want to share with you and help enrich your life. I want to pass on the knowledge I have learned over the years and share it with others.

Thanks again.

Check out my book site for other good books.
<u>Stevepease. net</u>

OTHER BOOKS YOU MAY BE INTERESTED IN

**Bass fishing boxed set
My 5 books to help you catch more bass.**

Do you want to know how to go on a new lake and catch bass like you fish it all the time? One of the toughest things for weekend Bass fisherman is knowing where to find fish. The problem comes when you fish a lake you have not fished before. Without the experience, you do not know where to fish unless you have a plan.

Kayak fishing, how to get started and set up your boat.

Kayak fishing is growing in popularity by leaps and bounds for many good reasons. Most of the reasons for the popularity are practical reasons that make sense.

Northern Pike Fishing

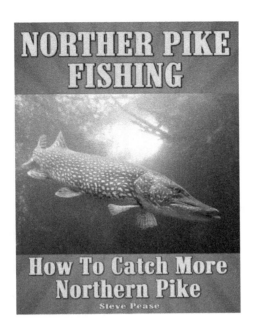

NORTHER PIKE FISHING

How To Catch More Northern Pike

Steve Pease

Why you should read this book.
This book does not cover every aspect of Pike
fishing. I wrote this book so you can take it with you
or read it the night before hitting the water. This is
so you can have all the best tips and techniques
fresh in your mind. It an easy read which will help
you remember all the best ways to catch Pike when
you get in the boat.

I read a saying that makes me think of catching
Pike. It said, "God let me catch a fish today so big
that when I talk about it later, I don't even have to
exaggerate its size." This is a possibility when

fishing for Pike almost anywhere they roam. Every cast you throw in Pike waters could get you hooked on the biggest freshwater fish you will ever catch.